THE INVENTION OF DREAMING

THE INVENTION OF DREAMING

POEMS

ED RUZICKA

The Invention of Dreaming
Copyright © 2026 Ed Ruzicka
First Edition

Cover art painting *Turn Out the Stars*
by Edward Pramuk

Cover design by Jacob Arms
William K. Lawrence, Editor in Chief
Published by Serving House Books
Lawrence Landing Company
Raleigh, North Carolina 27609
United States of America

www.servinghousebooks.com

Serving House Books is a proud member of

Independent Book Publishers Association
 and
Community of Literary Magazines and Presses

Paperback ISBN: 9781947175327

ADVANCE PRAISE FOR ED RUZICKA

"Between hard times and heartfelt delight, Ed Ruzicka's latest collection of poems *The Invention of Dreaming* finds a way to brim with hope. This book seduces the heart and mind with surrealistic revelations of a pandemic and the starkness passage of seasons where brotherhood and healing coexist with heartache and "the cleansing release of dreaming." We pass through "nagging reflections, worse than a houseful of aunts" to find a world where the poet urges us to "Honor everything we hear, smell, see, taste or touch," and to not let even a brother's death diminish "the least of our acts." Ruzicka uses a jazz pianist's arpeggios, bird songs and the wind to create an anthem full of compassion and humanity."

> — Mona Lisa Saloy, Louisiana Poet Laureate (2021-2023) and author of *Black Creole Chronicles*

"Ed Ruzicka's *The Invention of Dreaming* witnesses' extraordinary acts of compassion in poems that honor common experiences that poets often ignore. His vocation here, as in his day-job, is care. These are the poems that William Carlos Williams asked for: hands-on, tender but unflinching, written at the balance-point of celebration and elegy."

> — Rodney Jones, winner of the Harper Lee Award in 2003 and the prestigious Kingsley-Tufts Award and author of *Transparent Gestures* and *Salvation Blues*

"In the Covid and post-Covid landscape of these poems, Ed Ruzicka shows us by poem-after-poem how the world goes on but can be transformed by our love and concern for one another. This densely textured book is healing. Read *The Invention of Dreaming* to go on surviving your life in our fractured times."

> — Peter Cooley, Louisiana Poet Laureate 2015-2017, Professor Emeritus. Tulane University, author of *Accounting for the Dark*

Dedications

To my wife Renee who prepared and fed me what little I could eat while I was sick and who cared for me with gentle patience.

I am now and forever indebted to these writers who have helped me more than I can say:

Charles deGravelles, John Tarleton, Andy King, Ben & Eillen Shieber, Jeanne George, Randolph Thomas, Carolyn Ricapito, Jack Albert, Gary Beaumier, Marilyn Shapley, Clare Ruzicka, Jane Napolitano, Miriam Ruzicka, Michael Newell, Robert Wexelblatt and, my editor, Meg Freer.

The front cover painting "Turn Out the Stars" is the center piece of a triptych painted by Edward Pramuk. The triptych, was used to promote Southeastern Louisiana State University's "Bill Evans Festival" in 2002 and now can be seen in the university's music building.

CONTENTS

Came in on a Plane

The Invention of Dreaming   3
A Watch, a Knife and the Sea   5
Crow at Night   6
I Tell the Young Poets   7
Coming to a Theater near You   9
Breathe   11
Didn't it Pour   12
Lost   13
Cherry   15
One Cup   16
Five-Twenty-Seven through...   18
My Brother   19
Three Windows   22
When   24
Oblivion   26
Respite in June   27
Carolyn   28
Warblers, Ibis, Sparrows, Bittern...   30
Curmudgeon   32
This Dawn   34

Zeitgeist in a Holding Cell

The Post   37
Voluntary Slavery   39
In Memory of Ellis Marsalis   40
I Fall Asleep the Night Louise Gluck...   41
Attic   43
West   44

I Drink Coffee Slowly   45
Earrings   46
Prayer   48
Shadow and Want   49
I Can't Stop Listening to the Nocturnes   50
Once in Żelazowa Wola   51
Birth of a Ghost Rider   52
Naming Leaves   54

Zero

Zero   59
Poem to Address a Question...   60
Insinuations of Rain   61
Seventieth Birthday   62
Foraging   63
The Weight   64
If This Day   65
Daylight Savings during a Pandemic   67
Ann   68
Bell's Tongue   70
My Front Door   71
Someone Else's Daughter   72
Why I Haven't Retired (To Write)   73
Boxcars and a Hammer   74
The Second Last Day of the Year...   76
Horizon to Horizon   77
Off Shannon-Oxmoor Road   78
Sunsets Saturday Through Thursday   80
Promise   81
Beside the Wild Fire-pit   82
Dusk   84
Put the Stars Out   85

"I will show you fear in a handful of dust"

— T. S. Eliot, *The Waste Land*

"That one talent, which is death to hide, lodged with me useless ..."

— John Milton, *Sonnet on His Blindness*

CAME IN
ON A PLANE

The Invention of Dreaming

Look long at the scarred bellies
of sharks as their granite torsos
drag over empty parking lots.

Gray fins sweep down into tree tops,
twist branches above neighbors
who walk schnauzers, beagles, shepherds
because they have no work to go to.

Sharks nose down, press on
hospital windows while archangels
lean against respirators. Swords
slung off their hips, archangels yawn,
bored as camp soldiers awaiting orders.

The unseasoned nurses and the wrinkled ones,
cry, pray, curse. implore the Lord, implore whatever.
They cannot hug, cannot touch,
must maintain a six-feet distance.
Before they walk out of any room
they strip off pastel-colored gowns and gloves.

This is where dark angels swim under doorways,
pour down from heater vents to nibble
in the mucked-up backwater of lungs.

Dark angels shut out the lights.
They shut out the lights.

Since time immemorial, plagues,
predators, malevolence, storms
have torn at us. There was a day
when Yahweh's heart was turned
to pity. He rose,
he padded back to tinker
in his work room in the stars.

In a season like this season
he invented the cleansing
release of dreaming.

A Watch, a Knife and the Sea

Not eating enough, he wizened,
turned thin as a wrist watch,

had a time piece's
pale, sallow glow.

When he was able to stand
his shadow was a blade's shadow

where light only pauses
as its waves wash around.

In all of that pain he still
welcomed the shallow

pooling of breath beneath
a rib cage that lifted in tides.

Crow at Night

Obsidian night,
black water,
hunger.

A crow watches
the moon roll
dusk to dawn
with an inevitability
few of us reach.

At least not, the three
citizens of Baton Rouge
that were rolled into the city
morgue today on stretchers
to disappear into drawers.

Obsidian wind,
black hunger,
water.

Wind and anxiety nag
willow branches. Crow's
talons hold to a branch
over a tossing chainmail
of pond water.

From inside limbs
that light barely touches,
the crow watches a year
darker, even, than itself.

Obsidian night,
restless wind,
hunger.

I Tell the Young Poets

Wounds are how light finds its way in. —Rumi

Take walks, ride buses. It doesn't matter
where you go. Listen to Uber drivers.
Watch the way wind fiddles bush limbs,
plays with the feathers of birds.
Hear drums at work in the world.

Let breath rest inside your lungs
until you can fathom
how the universe transforms there,
is imbedded in blood to course out
through our arteries. If you speak
too hastily you could end like
too many old poets, lost
in a turmoil of your own words.

Attend to the least of acts: passageways
that open down the backs of cat's eyes,
the weight of a butter knife as it lifts,
how elevators breathe us in
and out and in, that rooms
do not exist until you create them.

Today's poem begins with a woman
that yesterday had a plastic tube down her throat
to do her breathing for her. She was tethered
to a half-dozen life lines and a machine
that erupted into alarms if her heart skipped.

The ICU nurse may go back to her computer
when an alarm sounds or the nurse may charge in
(Without a thought of her husband
and three children at home.) ready to do
whatever it takes to save a life.
Every nurse knows how little it takes
these days for anyone to turn into nothing
more than notes in a chart, ink on a shroud-white page.

But today this woman has a therapist at her elbow
that is helping her to experience the miracle of being
able to stand again and wash her hands
at a small silver sink five feet from an ICU bed.
I honor that. Honor everything we hear,
smell, see, taste or touch.

Coming to a Theater Near You

People are not quite dropping like flies.
Still, I don't envy my former neighbor Glenn.
Since last Thanksgiving Glenn's been
stuck in a wheelchair
beside a half-dozen other wheelchairs
in a linoleum floored sunroom.
At least that's where I find him
every other week when I visit.

We sit off to the side
as a guy the residents call
Crazy Charlie hocks up phlegm,
on-account-of Crazy Charlie
didn't have the smarts or will to quit
those little swizzle-stick cigarettes
he used to roll over his lips, contemplative-like
as he sat in the dugout shade
of a minor league ball diamond
thinking that with his speed, power and bat
he could get any broad in the stadium.
Just ask him, but keep your distance.

Once fear goes viral nothing's right.
The thing is, you don't want to be shelved
in a nursing home as the cable channels show
a man who actually makes himself look orange,
grouse on and on about how he has vanquished
the pandemic so it will never become
a horror feature playing in a theater near you.

The fact is everybody knows
they've got at least a bit part
in some ill-written scene
before this script ends
but instead of being listed
in any silvered, cellophane
roll of credits, too many of us
will end with our names
chiseled into granite.

Breathe

Neighbors I have never seen
walk dogs under our oaks.
Birds bob across lawns, jab at dirt.

A constellation of roses
gush blood-red into March.

There is an abundance
of tedium amid a million
unfilled hours. Eyes swim in
the aquarium light of screens.

Children cry for
crayons and bike rides.
Stoplights tell so very few
to come ahead or go.

Some grocery clerks
wear gloves or masks.
Some do not. There is
Plexiglas between the clerk
and me, as if one or the other
sleeps in a prison cell.

She puts an item in the bag.
What we never fully sense
is how closely death attends
the least of our acts

or what spirits
pass in and out
with every breath.

Didn't It Pour

after the rains
after all of the rain's

swirls   whips   beats
tumbles   needles   splats

legions of slick frogs
grind the gears of their larynxes

ratchet up through the forest a song
that is an anthem of their own

Lost

You sounded the fool when we left the room
where your husband mumbled, sweated on sheets.
Dick's eyes were evaporating by the hour.
Sister-in law, you told me how good the Lord
is to every little sparrow. You intoned it as if
psalms are a balm one rubs into wounds.

Was leukemia his celestial gift? Is paralysis
a heaven-hurled bolt through the spinal cord
that helps us how, Sarah, helps us how?
For months his illness was a shadow. We ate, slept
in shadow. We walked through layers of shadow.

Everyone felt he had suffered enough.
We were a strained degree of grateful
when death undid him. Now you are broken.
The whatzamagigit of your soul gave out
and the hardware store no longer carries that part.
You wander and wander through your mirror
trying on this bleak dress, that solemn sweater.

My brother has left you alone to drive
to the lawyer's office, sign successions.
My brother has left you in the bank vault
of his absence where you can sigh and sigh
in deafening silence, lock-and-key security.

I knew I was losing my brother. I did not know
you would not allow us a proper gathering to begin
to fathom what we may never be able to fathom.
No one knew that just a month after Dick
turned to ash everyone would suddenly
imprison themselves in their homes because
a virus had bought a ticket into the country.

We do not even know what vessel or cardboard
box holds our brother's remains. I did not know
I would lose you, sister-in-law, who decades ago
brought grace in through our kitchen door.

If we ask, you occasionally offer the family your
wounds, slip tiny razors off the end of your tongue.
You do give us one window onto how treacherous grief
can get and the cracked ice of your gaze.

Cherry

The flesh is dense,
fibrous. Skin
dark and thin.

Teeth and tongue
easily strip the meat.
The stone is round,
is pleasing to the mouth.

If split, the seed
is poison
except to earth.
Fruit of earth's bounty.

One Cup

Now that I am old
with an old man's problems,
my organs revolt against me.
I am allowed only
sips from a favorite cup
brimmed with dark drafts
on special occasions

like today which is Monday.
Special and fresh, Monday
sits in its own square on the calendar,
has been waiting patiently
while seven moons swept
over the crowns of our trees.

I grind beans, heat water
until a gauze of steam shimmers
in front of salt and pepper shakers.
I tip a spout of scald-hot water
into the paper filter, grounds.

I hold every mouthful
on my tongue
the slow way my hand
sometimes lingers
on your hip, your right shoulder
or at the base of your neck, my love,

while we are under stars.
While we drift into
yet another unmoored night
in a darkness which I may also
treasure soon enough
and for longer.

Five-Twenty-Seven
through Five-Thirty-Nine

Branches blur
stroked with the night ink
Zen monks brush onto silk.

Light seeps through, so that
Every object stands
like a thing apart, unto itself.

Gray, silver and dark
balance the way stars
in constellations
wheel in locked unison.
The air is a wan aluminum.

In darkness, a storm passed.
Now nothing is as heavy as it was.
Not bone, not blanket,
not the murk of any
recent dream. Branches
stretch into dawn. Hope
whistles at the window glass.

My Brother

I.

We propped you up,
brought you the best we could find.
"Nibble, chew, swallow," we urged
though we could see it all tasted like silt.

A veil slipped between our faces
and yours, shrouded our voices.
So, we poured words out like wine
spilled on a priceless rug
when the party has gone on too long
and no one cares about anything anymore
but wine and how to keep the party going.

When we left the room
silence wrapped you up
as you learned the sleep
of a stone among stones.

Those days you woke from revelry
in the courtroom of eternity
to plead your case, mumble fervently,
though all of the pertinent filings had been lost,
though all of the pertinent filings had gotten misplaced.
So, you were the first of us to find out,
my brother, what it is to be naked.
Naked in a drawer at the morgue.

II.

I have been left alone
to wander a landscape
where you, my brother, went
after you turned to stone among stones.

One can know how to weep
and not weep. My name is not Jesus.
My heart is not the heart of Jesus.
Brother, your name is not Jesus.
You are not getting back up.

III.

I am in a dark that will not end,
alone with your name
which is all I have left
after you turned to stone among stones.

I was with you when it started.
You were weak under covers in your bed
or sunken into the recliner in the living room.
That is when you began to leak light.

IV.

I know that our other brother
and our sisters are somewhere
but there is too much dark and stone
to find them – at least on this night
which has lasted for months.

For months my arms have seemed
too heavy to lift in this dark
in which we have been locked.
My feet have to feel for the path.
Your new mountainside
rises as close and cold
as a cave wall.

I have only this tongue of stone.

Three Windows

In my new ritual one palm
scours the other. Fingers
rub together bone down bone.
Windows of meditation open.

Since childhood my cousin Pam
has lightened every room she enters
but is now on her third round of chemo.
Pam lost one son to brain cancer.
A second took his life last Thanksgiving.
Pam's husband goes to the store for her.
Some days she is still good enough
to lift her brush, paint mountainsides,
dab flowers in along arroyos.
Covid holds her prisoner
in a ranch house.

I imagine a janitor who pulls a black
fifty-five-gallon drum on wheels
down a nursing home hall.
Mop handle, broomsticks jut up,
angles akimbo. A cough. A shuffle,
slow, then slower. Another cough.

My sister Mary who bent down
to nurse our mother through
her last three years now has
hatchwork lines etched into
her cheekbones.

The way dusk pans out
in the webbed backwaters
of a coastal marsh, light
seems to give up in the wrinkles
of Mary's face. In her senior's facility,
a dinner tray is left by her door.

Seattle, New Orleans, Boston,
Charleston gusts whisk
leaves into hospital doorways.
The atoms of chaos tumble,
until I wonder: which is it more –
what I do religiously, fervently –
hand washing or hand wringing.

When

It is hot. Our street,
the backyard, everything,
shot dead. I have driven
to the bank of a river.
I don't want to see anyone,
not even myself.

I am tired of all
the bickering in me,
those dozen-plus
little voices that chatter.
That try to set up
their small table
with chairs in my head.
Nagging reflections suggest
they know everything.
It's worse than
a houseful of aunts.

That's the thing.
I have seen enough
to be tired of what
everyone says is important.
I want it all at arm's length.

To stand just off
the cuff of tedium
while wind exhales
into river willow.

To stand within
wind's ceaseless knitting
of the landscape
as hidden in a deep
den of green
one bird chooses
when to sing the sun
and when not.

Oblivion

If I lay suspended
in the stillness of five a.m.,

parallel beside the question mark
of your abandoned bones
your turn   counter turn

to listen into the quell of an hour
in which interstellar wind
works in tree tops,

who should I have to confess to
that I no longer care
that my chest and ears

are no different than those
of a stag sunken deep
within the equilibrium of its forest?

Respite in June

Wind bends the shafts
        of banana leaves
or knocks them all together.

Rain tips camellia leaves
        taps, shifts its vowels.

Squirrels do the same things
        squirrels always do,
show the same
        tense twitches,
        acrobatic feats
above the diamond shivered yard.

Wind has gone into the next block.
It is better to listen than to move

Carolyn

Carolyn is nine hundred miles from our arms.
Her husband takes her temperature every hour.
Her skin has turned to a frail parchment
starlight tattoos with its needles.
Carolyn's ribs ached all night while an owl
forced the moon in and out of its chest.

Carolyn comes to our patio every summer
to flash blue eyes her mother gave her,
eyes we do not want diminished to mere mirrors.

Annually, Carolyn paints the shorelines
of Maine and Georgia
because she knows what it is to be fiercely alone
and is right now alone in the way she has always known
on a shore never advertised in travel magazines.

Carolyn drank sunlight from over our own
Mississippi River
as it made its way to be drowned and reborn
and drowned in the Gulf of Mexico
and then painted the river in oils on a canvas.

Carolyn also painted the white flower in a wine bottle
I pulled out of the garbage on Rittiner Street
when I went to visit one day after
she had tried to purge herself of delusions
the way young people will do when they ignite,
desperate to burn away any trace of their past.

Carolyn is with us every summer while sun
throws burning lances down and
we need her here again with her bottled water
and laugh that barely escapes swallowing itself.

She needs to be here again if we are
going to be able to go forward into
the landscape of all that is taken.

Warblers, Ibis, Sparrows, Bittern, Kingfishers

Even swaddled, Baby Henry wriggles
as if a worm works inside him.
He spits up onto a towel draped
over my daughter's shoulder.

I call Baby Henry "Killer" because his mother,
my daughter, is one of the new-minted
Fatimas, whose eyes flash above masks
as she whisks into patient's rooms,
attends them bedside, orders new meds.

Martin, her husband, is even more at risk
in the ICU where he has to force tubes
down sedated throats so a machine
can fill failed lungs. Both carry
the hospital home to wee-bean Henry.
Neither lets us within ten feet of our little pip.
No telling what might have found its way
into the frail birdcage of his ribs.

Renee and I stand on the lawn.
The three of them stay by the door.
Martin shows us what they call "Superman."
Martin puts Baby Henry, tummy down,
over his shoulder. Sleepy Henry stretches
halfway straight, maybe too dangerously close
to an unseen load of Kryptonite.

The next weekend we take the canoe out.
Oars on knees, wind nudges us under
cypress trees luminous as lettuce.
A yellow-bibbed bird lights, fluffs
six feet above Renee's shoulder. Maybe
a vireo, maybe a warbler? Let's go with vireo.
Back out in the lake we drift through dozens
of birdcalls, each an illegible signature
with its own set of quavers, dots, fades.

I barely know a handful. Maybe I'll recognize
more by the time I get young Henry into a boat,
row him around, teach him to keen
into the silence behind all the birdsongs
that will have gone extinct before he
learns to tune his own ears up.

Curmudgeon

I look forward to off elections
when candidates for judge and city council
mail out stiff fliers with their mug shots on the top side.
On the back, they stand stalwart with their brood,
backed by red white and blue. A lot of blue,
Prussian blue.

The paper is almost razor thin but strong
and bows well enough to sweep up shattered glass
cleaner than any store-bought dustpan.

My grandma taught me
to pinch a nickel, squeeze a dime.
Let nothing go in the trash bin
unless you're absolutely sure
it has no other use.

Bread ties can fasten folded extension cords. Worn
shirts can be scissored in strips to tie tomato stalks.
Keep safety pins in an emptied throat lozenge tin.
Line a small trash can with a bag from a Qwik-Mart.

Once folks didn't have much. Now we do.
I cling to the old ways, save what I can, paper clips,
plastic bags. Try to save the whale's baleens,
the bellies of ravens from plastics. Like grandma,

I live the way a mite does in a wall crack,
take great joy in being a curmudgeon
raised by frugal Czechs in a Midwest
where Februaries roar in like monsters
born in a Grimm's fairy tale
and fear our future might
come at us just that damn hard.

This Dawn

Grades of light filter
through ashen branches
framed in a blank window.

I drift out of dream
the way an astronaut
tethered to their capsule
floats, suspends.

The dark bay of the lungs
rises, sinks. rises.

These bones shed
that snowy radiance
seen only in x-rays.

ZEITGEIST IN A HOLDING CELL

The Post

They postponed all meetings until health.
Saturdays were canceled right away
or all days became Saturdays.
I can't tell which. Kid's birthday parties
are long parades of honking cars.

Band members play riffs
for couches and walls at random hours
in houses and apartments interspersed
throughout the city. Dancers
dance at the end of iPhones.
In Cleveland's Progressive Field bleachers,
cardboard fans shimmy in lake wind.

Many stay home frightened, have groceries delivered,
decide to wash everything but their infants in Clorox.
The president indicates it might be best practice
to swallow all the Borax you can find on store shelves,
see if surgeons can splice UV into bronchi.
There has to be a procedure for that.

We all have lots of time to watch a man
kneel on another man's neck for longer
than it takes to brew a proper pot of coffee.

All of our calendars are blank. It is as if
an Arctic vortex has dumped snow,
frozen 50 states March through August.

Too many see fatigued doctors, fatigued nurses
and decide to hit the bars, but the bars are closed.
The bars are in our living rooms. I am not
touching anyone, not even my grandchild.
I am telling you, I am postponed.

Mail has started to pile up in bins.
Most of us have a secret plan
to vote not to lose our lives.

Voluntary Slavery

I wear a mask for the man
who took shrapnel in a fox-hole
the day his buddy from Nevada
died in 1951, in a country whose language
neither one ever learned beyond the words
for price, bathroom and fuckie-fuckie.
I saw him today in the vegetable section
seemingly leashed off his wife's wrist, seemingly
clueless without her. A fine mist fell on her hands
as she tested zucchini for firmness.

I wear a mask for the nurse who once gave it up
to a guy home for the weekend from college
and who now has to shower and change –
get the ICU off of her – before she can hug
that child she has finally found a way to support.

I wear a mask as the cashier's
bones slump beside her register.
I wear a mask so fewer children's
alveoli will turn brittle and thicken,
restrict oxygen forced in by a machine.

Though it is hard to breathe
through a mask, I breathe easier,
just a shade easier.

In Memory of Ellis Marsalis

What is an arpeggio
that it sails
        so quickly –
                ear to heart,
resonates,
        heightens the instant,
                for as long
                        as notes last?

Back held erect,
        with calm authority
                you nurtured the keys.

There wasn't a song
        you couldn't take apart
                and put back together

transformed simply
        the way light bends
                a straight rod
                        underwater.

                In your hands
        in the movement of your hands
in the movement of your hands over keys

came arpeggios
        the soul did not know
                it knew.

I Fall Asleep the Night
Louise Gluck Wins the Nobel Prize
and Fires Consume the Cascades

She stands in the deep
of a half-denuded forest
amid sun-tortured timber.
The forest floor is tawny
and parched.

She is in a plain dress
she might have borrowed
from a museum tableau
where a Puritan family
reads the Bible by candlelight.

Louise Gluck's flesh
is waxy, sculptural
as she stands the way a hart
lightly sweating in the deep
of the forest stands,
poised, powerful, alert,
tender, vulnerable.

"It is time" she says,
"to scour the earth."
She opens her mouth
as if to let out a roar
but there is only the vast
silence of the forest.

Louise Gluck
starts to shake
like a machine
ready to fly apart.

She lights a match,
lets it drop at her feet.
Soon Louise Gluck shines
the way Joan of Arc once shone.

Attic

Shadows, joists, cobwebs.
Yesterday's gadgets.
Seasonal decoration, half-needed,
left to flounder in disorder.

Eight rolls of insulation laid out,
snug, and framed by floorboards.
More rolls still rolled up tight
like baled hay left too long
in the rain, sun and dew
in a field where bees swirl.

Unseen mice, mice droppings,
unbitten bait. Suitcases that sit
as barely visible dust motes
fall and swirl, soft as snow.

There is a top-of-the-line mixer
my ex-wife gave my eldest daughter
four moves ago for when she
has a home instead of an apartment
crowded with frustration.

There is an edgy tiredness here.
Everything is on the verge of obsolete
but still goes on, stays ready at hand,
not far off my pulse. What light
can make its way in is muddled,
washed dishwater gray.

West

fragile between
        tree branches
are those

the embers
        of day
        extinguishing

or the tinder
        of lovemaking
igniting

I Drink Coffee Slowly

Sky mussel grey with wedges
of a smeared blue. December,
bitter December. Steady needles
of rain tattoo my skin,
pepper the pavement.

This is what plants need,
splats small enough
to hold their spot,
be absorbed into soil, sink,
be taken in by thirsty pores
of rhizome and root.

Some flows off, sputters down
streetside gutters. Slender rills
gather in the veins of banana fronds,
swell till the leaf bows. A streak
flashes, brook-bright.

Which is to say that I have
nothing to do today
but balance out against
a front that pulls its hide
over half the state.
To feel what is tiny
and determined in me
work within what is
infinite, unflinching.

Earrings

Christmas came, or sort of did, and went,
with children in and out or previously committed.

A seventieth birthday floats towards you, my love,
another year looms like an iceberg, calved
and set adrift on the choppy seas of Covid
within the outward churn, the brood
of elements beyond our control.
All the elements are cold and coldly ticking.

Tyrannical winds, vectors, churlish brews,
and charged ionic clouds press their brows
against our frigid window glass.

As night disrobed, you disrobed.
Now as dawn puts on yesterday's clothes
you yank on your gray sweats
but also choose a pair of silver earrings
to ride your skin like bird notes.

Twin pins pierce lobes. You bear forth
toward two sunny side ups, toast.
I call this pride in the face
of what is faceless.

Above the sink, a blue geometry
of angles mingle in the indigo
bottle on the windowsill.
Three times you brew tea.

Thunder shakes from beyond
tree tops, down through timbers.
Lightning divides the oaks.

You go to the levelness
that surrounds chair and desk.
Later a warm bath, immersion
in dream and waking, waking
and dream, and dream and waking.

Prayer

In the morning, I slice strawberries into cereal,
turn my key in the Kia's tumbler, guide the car to work.
Around ten I uncap toothpaste for poor, addled
Mrs. Robichaux in room 654. After lunch
I teach a stroke victim how to manage
the one-handed shoe tie. In 631
I staunch blood from a surgical wound,
call in the nurse. Before I leave the hospital,
with practiced, precise movements,
I wash the day off my hands.

On the way home I stop at Vernon's hardware
and lift a tin handle, swing a gallon can of pitch
off the shelf. One clerk has a buzz cut, the other
has the flaxen locks Thracian warriors wore
when they hurled spears into Persian ranks.
(Both clerks have tattoos inked over biceps
and into the delicate skins of their forearms.)

While sunset flourishes between pines
I cradle a book on the patio.
I tap out a text to our youngest.
As I go to sleep, I pray that
a few times every day
my fingers can drip diamonds
the way the leaves of the Mexican petunias
dripped beads on Sunday after a torrent of rain.

Shadow and Want

Wind without feathers
other than the way
wind feathers dark water.

Moon of toothless skulls,
soundless howls.

The only nakedness except
the nakedness of hunger
is the nakedness of loss.

Moth wings fall apart, smudge
the parchment of my thumb.

Branches are bereft of birds
Throats without rush of whistles.

On a planet of hunger
I am bereft.

I Can't Stop Listening to the Nocturnes

Frédéric Chopin
whispered a spell
to lull history to sleep.

Stars drift within
the gyre of his galaxy
formed in C-Sharp Minor.

Morning stirs
as the pianist works
minor chord arpeggios,
into a horsetail churn.

From the patio,
I cannot see inside
branches and leaves
where one thrush calls
to another unseen thrush.

Against the invidious
math of Covid
that is our jailer,

deep in the lungs,
the piano's crystal notes
bond with oxygen.

In a solitary yard
nocturnes
are my medicine.

Once in Żelazowa Wola

Frédéric Chopin: Nocturnes

soft assault
       horsetail swirls
              whiffs
                    barrages

snow   drapes hills
       breathes and drifts
              under a teacup
                of moonlight

exquisite delicacy
       on black boughs
              silence falls
              on silence

a brook swallows flakes
       a wren shrugs
              blade
                of sunrise

the pianist drives snow
       from the fury of his heart
              fly
                crystals

Birth of a Ghost Rider

Yesterday I came across a postcard
of a bridge in Clearwater, Florida.
I think my dead brother and I
rode over that bridge once.

It was never about getting anywhere with Dick.
It was about becoming stronger, sharper.
You cannot get leaner or quicker
than the newly formed ghost I now envision
leading me over that bridge
and along a wind-whipped shore.

Brother, your downtown high-rise
had sixteen stories that looked over
the Saint Pete Marina, though
you barely even glanced that way.
We never went to the marina.
You took me to the stairwell
of your building where you routinely
hiked up flights of staircases.
As many as five sets of sixteen at a go.

You took me on monster bike treks.
When I stopped to watch a pelican
preen on a dock post, or parrots
whirl up into palm fronds,
you waited up ahead,
one cleated hoof on pavement,

the other fixed to its pedal, eager.
By the bridge, your silhouette thinned
then flamed out through heat waves.
As sand beaches baked behind you,
gulls dove between breakers.

Eldest brother, you were always
driven, obsessed. Death may have
already been over your shoulder
every time you went up that stairwell
to prove nothing over and over.
You can train for everything, except that.

Naming Leaves

Six days after the great ice storm
so chilling that it knocked fear of Covid
straight out of our brains,
I hold baby Henry in my arms.

We are in my daughter's backyard
and already engulfed in a soft,
spring turn of sky. An owl calls
from the recesses of a magnolia.

Baby Henry looks at a bush,
its leaves shriveled by recent ice.
He raises an arm, points a finger.
Says "Phooof." Shifts the finger
two inches, says "Vvuuu."

Now Henry turns his attention
to the wings of a fern.
He can't yet fully extend
that index finger. It curls
in the direction of a frond.

Eyes luminous as twin moons,
Henry focuses on a single leaf, says
"Tthaaa." Again, even softer, "Whough."

In the aftermath of the storm's destruction
Baby Henry has purposed himself
to naming, one by one, the leaves

and then, I guess, each grass blade,
every stitch of rain that falls
downward through his gaze

so that I might come to know them
as he does and to understand
how to turn any afternoon
into a slow benediction.

ZERO

Zero

This virus puts zeros in my eyes,
whispers deep as it slinks along
dank passages within the cochlea.

This virus presses hard on cell walls,
presses every cul-de-sac in my lungs,
deflates me the way machines
roll and stamp every molecule of air
out of plastic bags before they are enwrapped,
packaged, freighted and left for months
with dust, spiders and rodents on storeroom shelves.

I am in a bedroom alone
down a corridor of zeros.
Dawn can hardly find me.

I wait for an angel to budge
this round rock at the face
of this cave. The rock is another
zero heavy enough to inter me.

The days of my calendar
are empty windows
where dust has piled on sills.
The blue fly and the black
both buzz, both gum up the panes.

This is how it is in August 2020
in a small room down the corridor of zeros.
As others put boots in the street, I have to work
to lift a glass of water to the lips of zero.

Poem To Address a Question
No One Asked

Do I still feel
the dark star,
the one that imploded
not long after the birth of light,
the one whose abominable gravity
drew me toward it
at the base of my spine
at a pinprick deep inside me,
deep inside the prehistory
of the coccyx that imprints
in every coccyx of man, fish,
beast, bird and fowl?
Just barely.

For almost three weeks
the star drew in,
consumed me,
It has released me.

Last night I slept again
with my love in my arms.
Soon I will wake to drink and eat
because this skeleton
is not ready
to live off only soil,
obsidian and memory.

Insinuations of Rain

This front whirls,
roils like a child
let loose at the fair
to dash and spin.

Winds whip down.
Branches swoop this way, that,
in a symphony of monstrous chaos.

Tree chimes ring – bells of a ferry
that nods through thick fog.
Flower petals lift to sample
trace minerals in the air.

Every pore is poised for rain's arrival
as this city breathes like a lover
who has thrown aside the sheets.

Seventieth Birthday

Give me one,
give me one dram.

Night totters on the brink.
Give me one more dram
while crickets erupt into song.
.
Dragged across treetops
in the swill of sunset,
a shawl of saffron
inhales its own perfume

Just one dram.
Let darkness seal the rest.

One more dram amid
the thrum and threat
of crosshatched days.

Foraging

This day begins with an eastern sky
colored the same murk and mauve
I turned milk into by crushing blackberries
against the sides of a bowl with a spoon
during summer days that leaked into infinity.

My mother sent us out with dented colanders
dented pots. We crouched among stickers,
twisted the twigs of our young limbs craftily
through prickly branches to pluck
beaded berries off of stems,

left only a small platform, a sort of pock
at the end of each stem surrounded
by sepals, curled as lion's manes.

One to the mouth
for every four to the colander
under the shade of a forest
between our land and Triplet's.

It was a wild throng of bushes.
Crickets and cicadas screamed
as if nothing had changed for them ever
since the beginning of time.
Why, why, why did it ever,
then, change for me?

The Weight

It is incumbent upon me
to lie alone at the star point
where darkness begins
its turn toward day.

Love and lust
twine through me.
Aside from this pining
for your absent flesh
in the twisted fibers
of the dark

there is only
the slight weight
of dawn which rests
light as a lover's hand
on my chest.

If This Day

I go from room to room,
605, 523, 541, 556.
Shadows under the beds
do not move no matter who
mutters under the sheet:
retired pipe-fitter, sister-in-law,
woman who sang alto in the choir
at New Zion Baptist on Marigold St.

I go home to debt on the house, the car –
shamble of bills sliding off
the desk top. Ceiling tiles sag above,
exhausted, the way the tiles
gave up years ago and accepted
the roles humidity and decay play in our homes.

Debts of time that bones know
while the clock in the kitchen
seems to gain a minute a month.
Soft tics of morning, fog in the branches
as November engulfs the landscape.

Things lost in the backs of the closets
and only recovered by daughters
some day after the will is read,
after the backhoe dumps dirt
on the casket, another old soul
brought back to dust.

And the shadows of hunger in children's mouths
in rent houses I do not know
but know more of than I want to admit.

Couldn't it all blow off the way spores
whisked into wind those summers I rolled
in dandelions. I'd pluck green stems,
send dewy seeds off in wild shoots

let their silk catch along the rasp
of slender birch that lined the banks
of our town's brown, shifting currents.
White and tumbling, those downy seeds drowned
within our town's own, old-timeless river.
If this day were not so heavy, that.

Daylight Savings During a Pandemic

We are in this predicament
of being almost through to
the shortest day of the year.

Dawn stays lost on the other side
of hope. On a telephone wire
a dove preens shaded feathers.
A young woman, work dress sliced in half
by the cone of the street lamp light, curses
a flat tire. I hear her dial her dad for help.

Parked up the street, I rev
my engine, veer off.
Everything still happens,
just a little less of it now.

Even the sun has trouble hauling itself up
from the slop of waves. Over
a wind-tossed lake, the sun
is a brilliant streak. For one whole-note
the sun rests, too burdened to raise itself up
and assume the magnificence of its day.

Ann

Born in 1935
she worked up until
the time of Covid
when she got a pneumonia
that landed her in rehab

where she moves
through pearled fog and minutia
of her pain as if hope
pulls her along on a string.
Ann now sports a walker
that has two fluorescent,
yellow tennis balls
on its back legs.

Ann is so thin
that if you made
a pencil sketch of her,
then laid the pencil down on top
only these would stick out:
       splayed split ends,
       a bulge of sweater,
       butt curve, toes
       in gripper-socks.

Today she tells me
she keeps six horses
in a pasture above Pride, LA.

She hopes
to saddle up again.
Hopes at least
to feed them from
her open palm
the way she always has.
Apple slices, carrots.
Wants to share
at least a few more
honey buns.

Bell's Tongue

I go back inside. Because
you have gone half-blind,
I take your hand, lead you
out to our empty street.

Brown, crimson, jasmine
crinkled leaves drift down
from crepe myrtle along the drive,
collect in the gutter like the world
is becoming old around us.

I show you a new moon
low on the horizon –
a curled shaving of excelsior,
bell's lip, curve of light
at rest on a pregnant belly.

Moon's crescent cradles
an ashen sphere atomized
by atmospheric motes and gases
as light descends to these
round eyes I use
for everything and you.

Together we feel
how the moon's swell
will take over the sky
by the time we lie down
in our bed of blood and darkness.

My Front Door

Everything froze during a Polar Vortex
in the first year – or is it, maybe
the first decade – of Covid.
An ice storm cracked branches.
Electrical lines snapped, fell into the streets.
Power down, the inside temperature matched the out.

My front door stands closed
and dumb as a tree. Its brass knob
is silent and lonesome.
We use the back. There is a little light
the size of a thumbnail beside
the front door that no one goes to.
A dusky, ruby light for a doorbell
that does not ring.

One Halloween I forgot to lock
that door. A year later when I went
to put candy out in a bowl there,
I found the door had stayed unlocked
an entire year without anyone
even knocking in a place
made to be left alone.

Someone Else's Daughter

She is scrawny the way a day or a month can be
not much. The wind blows its load of bitter
against her hard. Tears at her clothes.

Behind a Quick-Stop, she is alone
with the look of having been alone
for some time. She stands beside
a marine-blue, paint-chipped dumpster
made of welded steel and lifted twice a week
on steel arms, gear-driven and capable of grinding
a man's finger or forearm to pulp if it gets in the way.

A Norther baffles and rips at her jacket,
bores into its batting. She is still young enough
that her spine is straight, her manner
determined, self-contained though she obviously
lacks direction. Twice she starts right,
and once left but ends where she starts. Maybe
her mind has to cross out whatever possibility
those directions, those decisions hold for her.

So, she stays suspended as I hold the gun handle
of a gas pump, load 15 gallons of petrol.
I am on my way to Target.
She is alone in a rage of wind.

Boxcars and a Hammer

3:52 a.m. arrives
          like a boxcar
with the boxcar of 3:53
          nowhere in sight

within the whirling gyroscope
          of darkness that spreads
 in every direction
          this frigid 3:52 a.m.
rains down
          ten-penny nails

what is different about
          3:52 is how a storm
that whacks house-boards
          turns night into
a hammer
          a hammer

Why I Haven't Retired (To Write)

For Lauren Clancey

In Room 556
the patient is a dollop
slumped and crumpled into a ball
under sheets. She is on her side,
forehead pressed to the bed rail.

When we begin to straighten her legs,
she lets out blood curdling screams.
As if we had no ears, we maneuver
stiff, cramped limbs.
Fluid comes back into her joints.
Then she understands
we will not be rough with her.

We lift her to sit
on the side of the bed.
We lend her support
around the shoulder girdle.
Her gaze fixes on floor tiles.

For a few minutes this woman
does not even raise her head or eyes
to look at her husband of forty-one years
who is the one who does
every tender thing for her.
After a few minutes she begins
to respond. "Yes," she nods,
she is alright. "Yes," she nods,
she wants to sit a little longer.

After we pivot her back down
this mother of three, this wife
starts to speak, gives her husband
her first words in four days.
As we align shoulders, hips, legs,
she lets us move her limbs as freely
as the cotton limbs of a child's doll.
Light is in the woman's face again.

I have never seen a poem
do as much good as work.

The Second to the Last Day
   of the First Year of Covid

Is this hell leaving or hell coming?
Few of us have anywhere to be.
Our lives suspend in the middle
of a calendar in which each square
holds only anxiety and fear.

A full moon floats at the end
of a street graded in grays –
steel to ash. The dawn is bleak
but has a few glimmers

the way even the oldest, most
banged up and ill-treated, aluminum
trash can catches bits and shreds
of moon. Barks light back out.

This day is a street I don't even
want to go down, an article half-read,
half absorbed in a waiting room where
I sit, detached, distracted, gnawed at by threats
on a December day when the thermometer
is expected to go down and up and down.

Horizon to Horizon

I drink   black wind
its edge   width

and height   stars churn
in dark quadrants

grass   grasses   blade upon blade
glisten fine as mohair

shush and whisper
of air between blades

soil teams with minerals
mites   grains   ants

long and long   I drink
and am myself consumed

Off Shannon-Oxmoor Road

Every few minutes headlights
sweep the highway. The moon is down.
Why do my feet fix here,
before the locked door of a white-wash church?
Pine boughs, jimsonweed and wild oat
bend in wind. Thousands of crickets sound.

I do not want to go in, have no need
for sanctuary. The pews are empty.
The leather covers of hymnals
are, no doubt, soft, having been oiled
by hand after faithful, searching hand.

This wracked asphalt parking lot
only fills on Sundays. Weeds have
forced themselves up through cracks
in the pavement. Like faith,
some things don't need much to grow.

Which is what I am feeling here,
a man who has wondered more than once
if Jesus should be held responsible
for all the travesties and bloodshed
committed for centuries in his name.

Decades ago, the congregation raised
this church. They poured their blood into it
to make it look the same as churches
they knew back in the old country
where they were baptized among kin.
Under Georgia pine, the church lists to the right.

More recently, another generation of men
added the long gangway of a ramp
so that the weak and the infirm
have a way to make it in, sing hymns.
I stop. I bathe in all that effort, all that faith.
It is dark. The crickets stay on after me.

Sunsets Saturday through Thursday

Three times apple-skin-green,
that band of the prism
one grade above lime,
atomized and slowly failing.

Twice, the yellow parchment
of a crone's wrist, with a crone's
characteristic purpling below.
The quickly aging evening
bruised to the north
between sprays of pine needles
in a neighbor's branches.

Later the moon is murky –
melting ice under a paper towel.

Wednesday a mist of orange,
soft as shafts that fall
through church glass.
Branches thrashed in black wind.

Then tonight, atop a wobbly
pinwheel spun out of the west,
slow-mo of a dryer window's turn:
silk chemise in a crimson streak,
wedge of watermelon, worn, maroon
tee in the shape of Tennessee,
towel pale, pale yellow.

Promise

new moon
slung West

slim sickle
alabaster

pocked rind
night its fruit

parenthesis open
to tomorrow

Beside the Wild Fire Pit

Dishes have been
rinsed and racked,
checks were inked,
slid into envelopes
to prop the month back up.

House by house
windows blank.
Black branches
creak in wind.

Renee and I are free
to be out on the patio
for this final blaze
of spring.

If I turn still as stone
while our fire roars
its furious heat
up a narrow chimney

know that I have not
abandoned you, have only
slipped into a state
where the dead come close.

Your sister lifts hands of need
from her side. The bulldog
we lost last fall curls at our feet again.

My brother was taken, erased.
Yet through memory, he tries to show
what I might do to make things better.
His heart is still that good.

It is a balance we have to reach,
the dead even with the living.

Dusk

Ink pools under bushes.
Blood-stained scarfs, mink shawls,
reflect in the stem of my gimlet's crystal.

As lavender clouds gather,
I grow weightless as a child
with a child's quicksilver soles.

What has left me
are the clouds of trouble
that piled inside my chest,
a tripled brood. One,
my ailing sister. Two,
my eldest brother's death.

Three, worry about Renee as she
moves through our evening kitchen,
fridge to counter, to stove.
Renee's eyes turn more murky
each year, as if the world
is trying to leave her.

Tonight, these frets lose their grip
as thunderclaps above
pull west, by mandate
of a regal sun.

Put the Stars Out

For Edward Pramuk

Listen to the piano
I carried down to the river.
River of snow and indifference.

River that takes away.
River that washes
what was.

Listen.
With every note
a star appears.
When the damper
petal is pushed, a star
implodes, a star grows
dense and dark.

As the deeply blue river
flows through night,
night's snow and night's
black holes, the piano
plants footprints into snow,
a trail back to where
dark stars once shone.

All of the disappeared stars
have a gravitational force
that bends the paths of light
in an indigo sky.

Because it is icy, because
it is cold, cold and empty,
you give me a tiny moon
even more slight than
the thought of a dime.

You also give the river
a second, dime-slim moon.
Now there are twin eyes
to see the talcum, blue snow
around the piano and the great
indigo darkness above.

To see how light is bent,
there are twin eyes.

Acknowledgments

"Lost" first appeared online in the *Rat's Ass Review*

"Carolyn" was published in the *Poeming Pidgeon's* quarterly web magazine.

Silver Birch Press released "Warblers," "Ibis," "Sparrows," "Bittern," "Kingfishers" as part of their *Thoughts on the Earth* series.

"Curmudgeon" also appeared online thanks to Silver Birch Press during their *How to Heal the Earth* series.

The Jerry Jazz Musician website was kind enough to post "In Memory of Ellis Marsalis."

"Zero" was shortlisted for the Zeitgeist Award by Willowdown Books and was part of their *Human to Human Anthology*.

"Naming Leaves" was part of the Spring/Summer issue of *Rat's Ass Review* recently released this year and also appeared in my third book, *Squalls*.

Verse Virtual gave a page to both "My Front Door" and "Ann" in one of their monthly web releases.

"Why I Haven't Retired to Write" was released in *Pure Slush's Work* volume 3, segment 5 of their *Life Cycles Series*.

"Sunsets Saturday Through Thursday" was first published in *The Charleston Anvil*.

The Vincent Brother Review first released both "Birth of a Ghost Rider" and "Beside the Wild Fire Pit."

THE AUTHOR

Ed Ruzicka has published three full-length books of poetry, most recently, *Squalls* (Kelsey Press, 2024). Ed's poems have appeared in the *Atlanta Review, Chicago Literary Review, Rattle, Canary,* and have received Pushcart nominations. Ed, who is also the president of the Poetry Society of Louisiana, lives with his wife, Renee, in Baton Rouge.